Contents

Let's fight fire

When an emergency call reaches the fire station the **firefighters** spring into action. Poles are a fast way down. Then they jump into the waiting fire engine and pull on their **uniforms**.

Ready for a quick change
The firefighters' protective uniforms are always left ready to pull on, with the trousers over the boots. It means they can get dressed in seconds.

First the firefighter climbs into the boots.

Next he pulls up the thick, fire-resistant trousers.

He is dressed and ready to go in just 30 seconds!

4

Fire! Fire!

On their way

Once all of the firefighters are aboard, they drive to the fire as fast as they can. That's when you hear the engine's loud siren.

Turntable ladder fire engine

Reflective strips will show up in thick smoke.

It's a fact

🚒 In a major city, a fire station may respond to more than 7,000 calls a year.

🚒 Between 4 and 10 firefighters can sit in a fire engine's cab, depending on its size.

Down to work

At the site of a fire, the firefighters begin to unload and connect **hoses**. Some hoses pick up **water** from hydrants. Others are used to spray water over the fire.

Hydrants act like taps to the main water supply. In some countries they can be seen on the streets.

Keep on pumping

A fire engine acts as a pump, pushing water through hoses to the firefighters. The fire engine pumps the water so powerfully that two or three firefighters may be needed to control just one hose.

Old methods

The earliest firefighting tool was a bucket. It was not a good way to fight fire. This leather and wood bucket was used over 300 years ago.

Many fire engines carry more than 480 metres (1,600 feet) of hose.

At the scene

All sorts of machines are called out to a fire, from fire **engines** to **ambulances**. Sometimes you may spot a fire **chief's** car.

Circular saw

Jaws of Life®

We have the power!

Some of the firefighter's tools are power-assisted. Here, a huge saw helps a firefighter to get into a building, while the Jaws of Life® are used to prise open a car.

Hydraulic platform fire engine

Around the world, the fire chief takes charge of the crews at a fire.

Fire chief's car

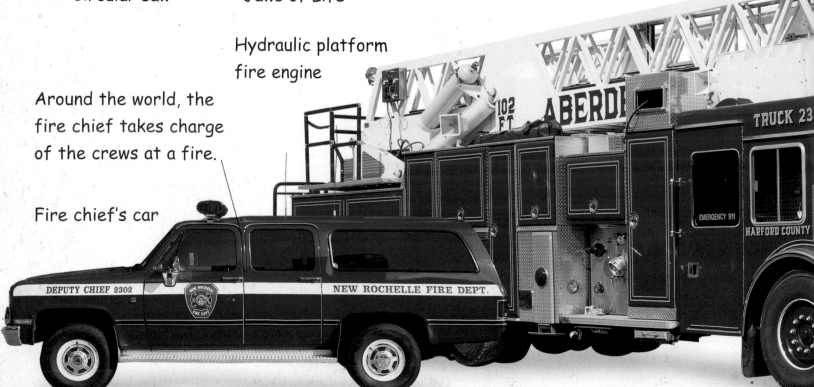

DEPUTY CHIEF 2302   NEW ROCHELLE FIRE DEPT.   ABERDE...   TRUCK 23   EMERGENCY 911   HARFORD COUNTY

An open house

A fire station is on call 24 hours a day. This means that there's always a team of firefighters ready to respond to an emergency call.

Water power

The most important firefighter's weapon is water, and the fire engines may have to pump huge amounts of water to put out a fire.

Up the ladder

Fire engines that carry telescopic ladders are used to observe and fight fires from above and to rescue people.

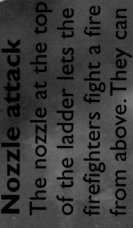
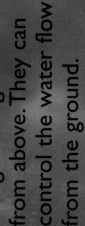

A hose runs up the ladder to the platform.

Nozzle attack
The nozzle at the top of the ladder lets the firefighters fight a fire from above. They can control the water flow from the ground.

Step onto the platform...

Some fire engines have a platform at the top of the ladder. People can step onto this from a building and step off at ground level.

The platform can be raised to the height of a seven-storey building.

...or use a ladder

A turntable ladder extends up a long way. This one will rise 32 metres (105 feet). The bottom rests on a turntable that can turn the ladder in a full circle.

Water works

The most familiar fire engine is a **pumper**. Pumpers carry huge water **tanks** and hundreds of metres of hose. Most importantly they have a powerful **pump**.

All pumped out
Pumpers are usually the first to reach a fire, and their crew will quickly find the nearest water supply. This might be a hydrant, or a pond, stream, or river.

A never-ending task
Following a fire, each hose has to be rolled up. The hoses are made of rubber-lined plastic so they don't rot.

Water intake valve

Hey! We Didn't Start the Fire

U.S.R.F.D.

Where do you need it?

In rural areas there may be no hydrant. The firefighters deal with this by setting up a portable tank. This will be filled with thousands of litres of water from water tanker trucks.

A pumper pulls, or drafts, water out of the portable tank and sends it on to the firefighters.

The tanker fills the portable tank in about three minutes.

Pumpers have to carry at least 13.5 metres (44 feet) of ladders.

Equipment is stored in lockers.

Water intake valve

ENGINE 1231

13

To the rescue

Rescue units carry more tools and equipment than other fire engines. They are called out for all sorts of reasons – and not just for fires.

Rescue units often have a control room inside.

The power of air

This rescue vehicle is being used in a training exercise with a mock traffic accident. The firefighters are using an air bag to lift the car.

An air line runs from the rescue vehicle to a control valve.

The firefighter controls air flow to the two air bags. Each has its own air line.

Air line

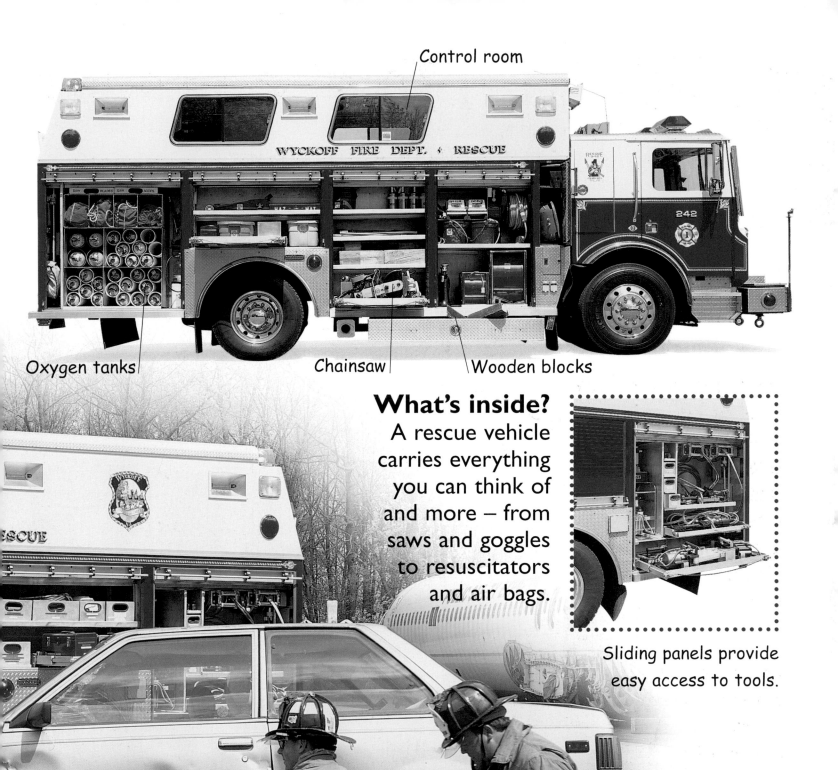

Control room

WYCKOFF FIRE DEPT. ✦ RESCUE

242

Oxygen tanks

Chainsaw

Wooden blocks

What's inside?
A rescue vehicle carries everything you can think of and more – from saws and goggles to resuscitators and air bags.

Sliding panels provide easy access to tools.

Air bag

Wooden blocks are used to support the car as it rises.

Wooden block

15

At the airport

Large **airports** have their own fire stations. An airport fire engine is very **powerful**, and carries more water and foam than an ordinary fire engine.

Airport firefighters wear fireproof silver suits.

Water control

As well as using hoses, the firefighters can direct streams of foam onto a fire from the two monitors on the cab. These are controlled from inside the cab.

Monitor

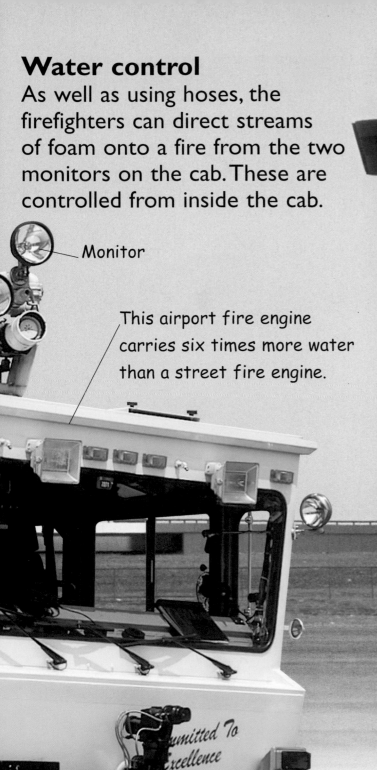

This airport fire engine carries six times more water than a street fire engine.

Monitor

Heavy-duty fire attack

Airport fire engines are so heavy that they need huge wheels to support them — but they can still reach 80 kph (50 mph) in 35 seconds!

17

Air attack

When fire breaks out in a **forest**, the best way to fight it is from above. A firefighting **plane** will drench the fire with water again and again.

Down for a pick up...
The plane swoops down to fill its tanks from the surface of a lake, a river, or from the sea.

...and off
The plane takes just 12 seconds to complete its sweep across the surface of the water. Its tanks are now full.

18

At top speed the plane travels more than three times as fast as a car on a motorway.

Before the water is dropped, it is mixed with foam to help smother the flames.

Firefighting

A firefighting plane can get to a fire safely from above, and normally reaches a fire much faster than a ground crew. This is important as a forest fire spreads incredibly fast.

19

Monster attack

Huge firefighting planes called **airtankers** are used to drop thousands of litres of fire retardant on **forest fires**. This helps to slow down the fire.

Back at base

The retardant is a red liquid that slows down and cools a fire. It is mixed up on the ground before being pumped into the air tanker. Workers handling it have to wear breathing equipment.

Why is it red?

The retardant contains a red dye to make it show up, so that the firefighters know where it has fallen. It soon fades.

Huge doors open to release the retardant.

This plane can carry and drop 11,300 litres (2,500 gallons) of retardant.

Danger flight

The pilot has to fly in very dangerous conditions, while keeping to the flight line. After a drop, the plane will head back to base to refill its tanks. This might take an hour.

It's a fact

There are different types of airtanker. All of them are converted from old military planes.

Rotor brigade

Helicopters are useful firefighting weapons, especially for fires that break out in remote, wooded areas.

On its way...
A helicopter may first ferry ground firefighters to a spot near the fire. It will then collect water from a nearby lake or river and return within minutes.

The bucket can be used to pick up water from very shallow lakes.

...and down it goes
A helicopter will hover near to a fire before dropping its water load. More than 1,000 litres (220 gallons) of water floods down onto a fire's hot spot.

A mighty thirst

This helicopter, known as a
Helitanker, sucks up water through
a hose called a snorkel. It sucks
quickly, filling its 9,500-litre (2,000-
gallon) tank in just 45 seconds. It can
drop the load in just three seconds.

The snorkel
acts just like
a big straw.

It's a fact

A helicopter may make up to
14 drops each hour, depending on
how far it is to the nearest water.

The Helitanker's water can be
dropped as a mist or in a torrent.

On the water

If a fire breaks out on a ship, or in a harbour-side building, **fireboats** and **tugs** are used to help put it out. They have an unlimited supply of water!

If the ship doesn't sink, the remains will be towed back to port and either repaired or broken up.

Use that tug

Large harbours use sturdy tugs to help guide ships and barges in and out of port, or tow broken-down boats to a mooring. Tugs are also valuable firefighting machines.

It's a fact

Tugs look small, but they are powerful – the engines have the power of about 25 trucks.

Tugs can move ships that are thousands of times their own weight.

With all monitors working, a fireboat can pump about five times the water of a fire engine.

Let's celebrate!
Fireboats can also be used to celebrate events. Shooting their water cannons, or monitors, at full power, they look very impressive.

In control
Fireboats have a number of monitors. These can be operated from the bridge or by hand.

Water jets can reach 90 metres (295 feet).

Foam is mixed with the water to fight oil-based fires.

Training day

Safety, fire behaviour, dangerous fumes...firefighters have a lot to learn. In many countries they do this at special training **schools**.

Fire it up!
Instructors use computers to control the fires at this US training school. They can control the spread and the height, and even put out a fire if necessary.

Extinguisher action
This replica steel car is used to train firefighters how to deal with a car on fire. An extinguisher is used to spray a chemical powder, starving the fire of oxygen.

The smoke looks bad, but these fires release no dangerous fumes.

Dressed in silver
Here the firefighters are directing a high pressure hose on a mock aircraft fire. Airport firefighters have to wear fireproof silver suits.

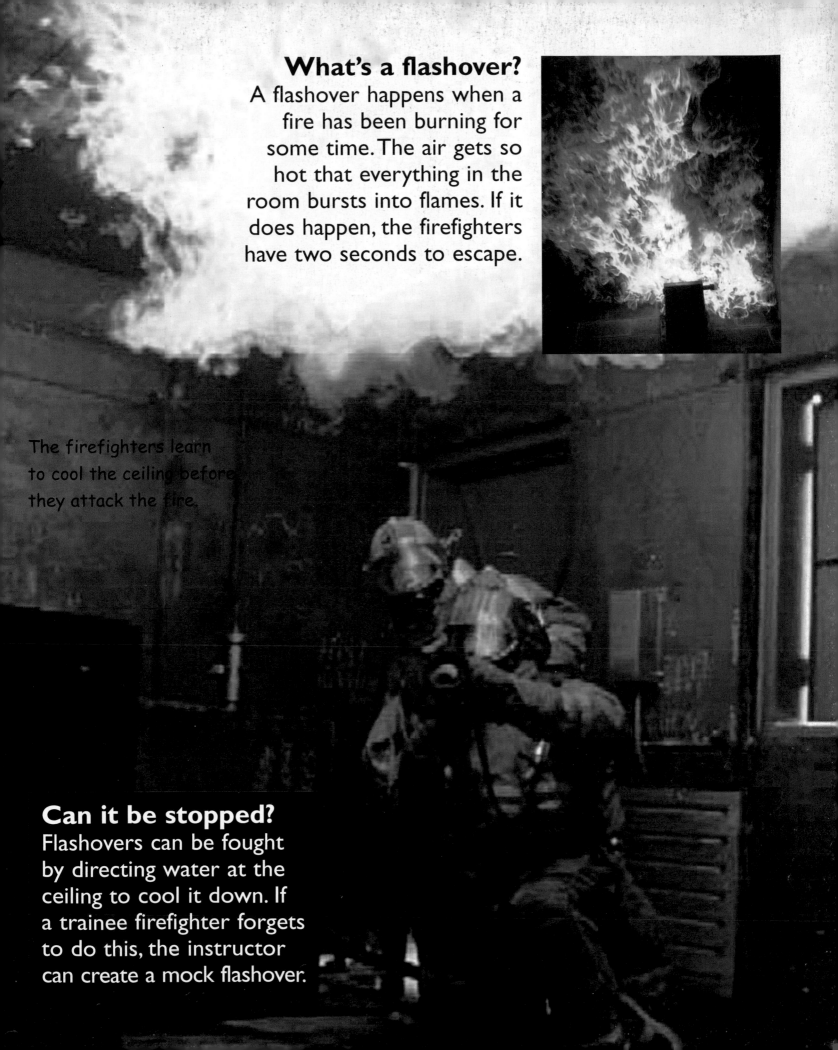

What's a flashover?
A flashover happens when a fire has been burning for some time. The air gets so hot that everything in the room bursts into flames. If it does happen, the firefighters have two seconds to escape.

The firefighters learn to cool the ceiling before they attack the fire.

Can it be stopped?
Flashovers can be fought by directing water at the ceiling to cool it down. If a trainee firefighter forgets to do this, the instructor can create a mock flashover.

Days of old

The **sleek** firefighting machines and the equipment of today are very different from the firefighting **machines** of old. The main difference is in the **power**.

Hands to the pump
In the 1700s fire engines pumped by hand came into use. This two-person pump would have delivered the power to pump a garden hose.

Each handle was pulled down in turn.

Hand-powered pump

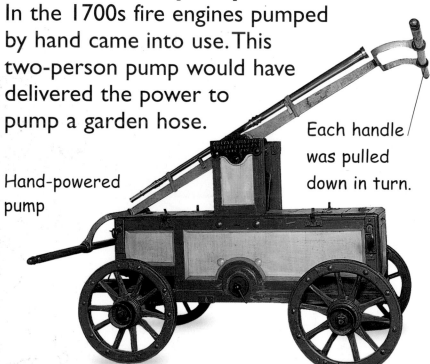

Horse drawn
Steam pumpers were drawn by teams of horses. The horses were trained to respond to the station's bell.

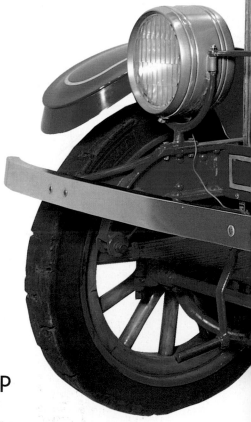

Steam pumper fire engine

Steam chimney

All steamed up
Steam power provided more water flow from the hoses. This pump dates from 1901.

Put it out!

Fire extinguishers have been used for many years. In the mid-1800s one method used the reaction of soda and acid to force water out.

Soda-acid extinguisher

Hand-pump extinguisher

Fire engines always carry alarm bells or sirens.

Muffin bell

Sound alert

Hand-held bells were once used to warn people of a fire.

Early 20th century TT Ford fire engine

Motor power

With the invention of the car, fire engines speeded up. The extra power also allowed them to carry more equipment.

29

Picture gallery

Firefighting aeroplane

The number of drops a
scooping aeroplane can make
depends on the distance to
a suitable water source.

Rescue unit

There are different kinds of
rescue units, depending on
what sort of rescue is
needed in the local area.

Fireboat

This fireboat's
engines are ten times
as powerful as those
on a fire engine.

Hydraulic platform

The highest hydraulic
platform currently
available can reach
the 33rd storey.

Turntable ladder

Water can be sprayed
from the ladder hose at
the rate of 3,785 litres
a minute.

Pumper

Pumpers are usually the first fire engines to leave the station.

Fire chief's car

A fire chief's car may be used for visits to local schools or businesses.

Firefighting helicopter

This helicopter can pick up water from a water source that is just 45 centimetres (18 in) deep.

Old fire engine

Firefighters clung on to the sides of early fire engines, standing on steps called running boards.

Airport fire engine

This fire engine carries a heat-seeking camera on top of the cab. It pinpoints hot spots inside a burning aeroplane.

Glossary

Air bag a bag that can be blown up to raise and support a vehicle.

Breathing apparatus the oxygen bottle and mask that a firefighter uses to breathe when there is smoke.

Control room an area inside a rescue unit that can be used by the fire chief.

Flashover this happens when the heat of a fire sets fire to other items in a room.

Hydrant this is like a huge tap to the main underground water system. Hydrants are sometimes seen in the street, or can be underground.

Hydraulic platform a fire engine with a long, extending arm that can be raised, with a platform on its end.

Jaws of Life® a tool that is used to cut open vehicles if anybody is trapped inside.

Monitor a powerful water cannon, used to spray water over a fire.

Nozzle the bit at the end of a hose, where the water or foam comes out.

Pump a device for drawing liquid along a tube.

Retardant a red liquid that slows the progress of a fire.

Resuscitator this is carried and used by an ambulance or fire crew to help revive a casualty.

Siren a device which produces a loud noise to warn people that a rescue vehicle is nearby.

Telescopic ladder a long ladder that folds up into itself.

Turntable ladder some ladders have a turntable at the base to allow them to be turned in a circle.

Tugs these strong boats are used to guide and tow larger boats. They are also used to fight fires.

Index

1926 fire engine

Acknowledgements

Dorling Kindersley would like to thank:
Fleur Star for preparing the index and assisting with the glossary.

Picture credits:

The publisher would like to thank the following for their kind permission to reproduce their photographs:

a=above; c=centre; b=below; l=left; r=right; t=top;

Agence France Presse: 19c, 23c; alamy.com: Simon Stock 3b; A.T. Willett 22r; Courtesy of Bombardier Inc: 18cl, 18cr, 30tl Bombardier Aerospace, Bombardier 415, SuperScooper, Multi-Purpose Amphibian are trademarks and/or registered trademarks of, and www.superscooper.com is a domain name belonging to, Bombardier Inc.; Carmichael International: Manchester Airport 17br; Corbis: 16bl; Emergency! Stock: Howard M. Paul 12bl, 13tr, 13tl; Firepix International: 8cr; Getty Images: Derek Berwin endpapers; Hulton Archive 26tr; PhotoLink 11c; Taxi 16 bkg; Jurgen Vogt 8br; Richard Leeney: Bergen County Fire Academy 12r, 14tl, 14c, 15tr, 15cr; NY Fire Museum 26tr, 26c, 26bl, 27tl, 27c, 32b; Museum Of London: 7tr; 911 Pictures: 7b, 18tr; NRE: 20cl; Rex Features: Today 22l; Tom Story: 20b, 21c; Superstock Ltd: 2c, 6c, 25c.

All other images © Dorling Kindersley
For further information see: www.dkimages.com